STANDARD 10-NOTE KA

MW01608884

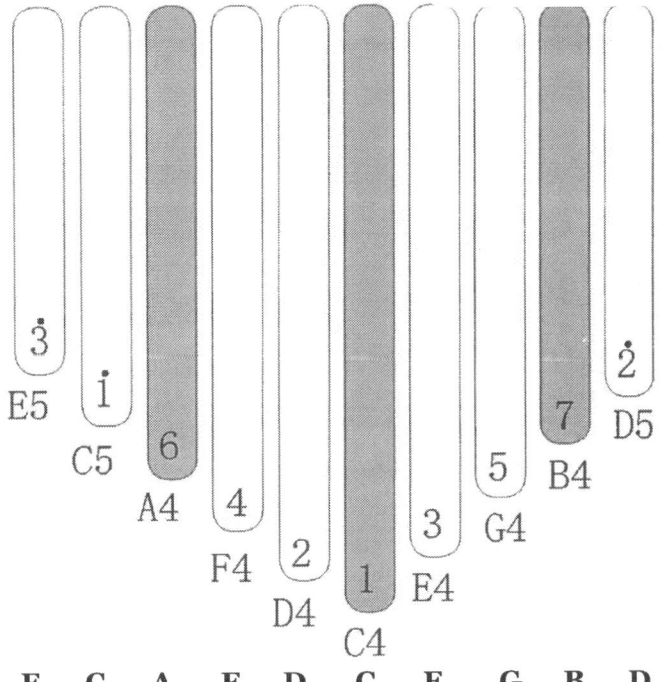

On most 8-10-tine kalimbas, the center tine will be a C note.

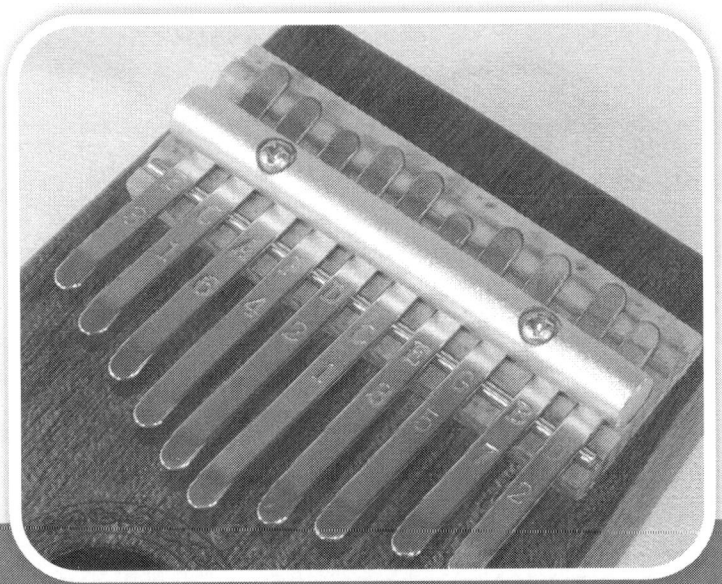

STANDARD 17-NOTE KALIMBA IN C SCALE

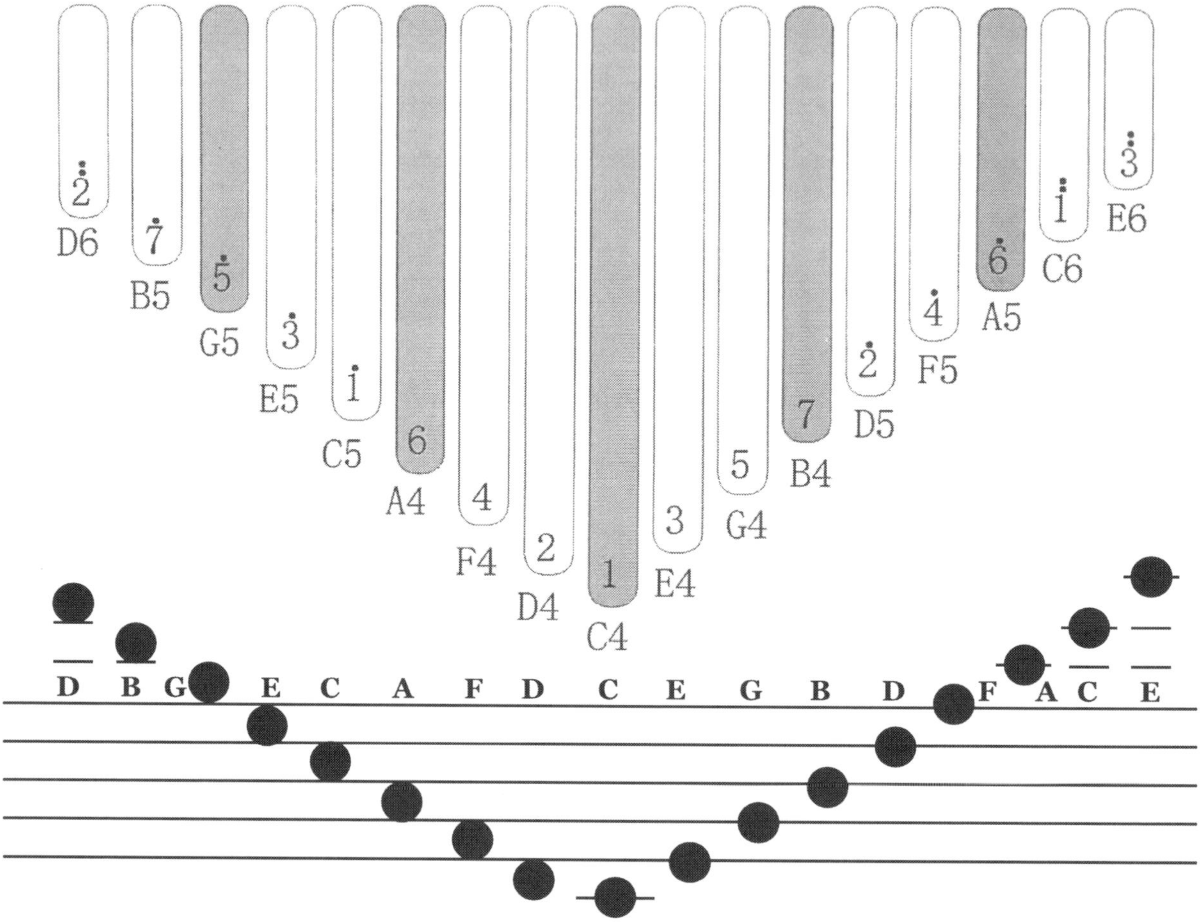

TUNING

If you want good sound, you must tune the keys. You can either use an entity tuner, or you can download a tuner app from your mobile phone. Android System app: gstrings, VITALtuner, Cleartune, and iStrobosoft.

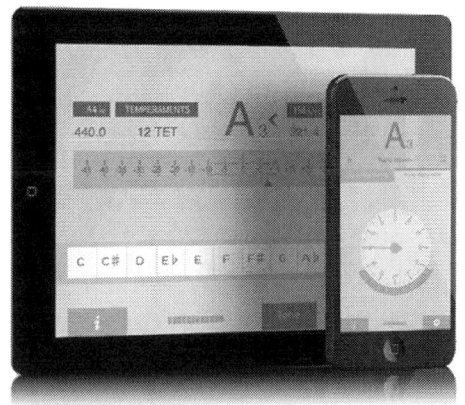

Note: Sometimes the tuner is not sensitive to the keys in the high-pitched position. There may be resonance when you first start playing. Press the keys nearby softly, and then tune your kalimba.

BUZZING SOUND

Occasionally, the keys make a slightly buzzing noise.
If this happens, simply move the keys left and right softly.
If this doesn't work, just place a paper card between the key
and the bridge to solve the problem.

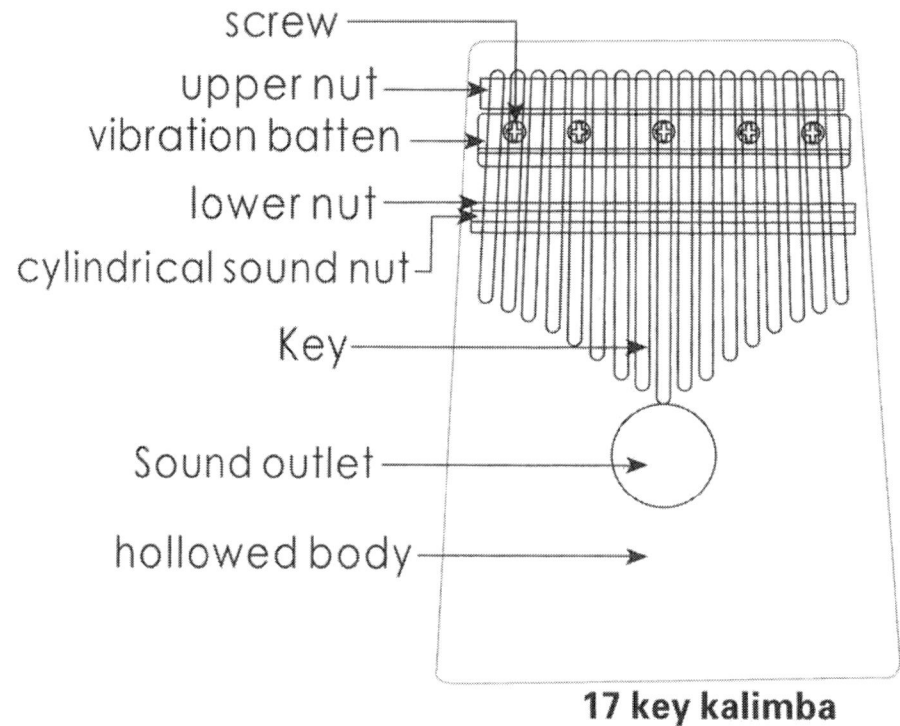

screw
upper nut
vibration batten
lower nut
cylindrical sound nut
Key
Sound outlet
hollowed body

17 key kalimba

CARE FOR YOUR KALIMBA

When not playing the kalimba, please store it in the bag.
Please keep your kalimba at a relative humidity level of
between 30 to 60 percent. If the kalimba gets damp, rust can
cause problems with the resonance of the keys.

HOW TO HOLD AND PLAY YOUR KALIMBA

- Hold the kalimba with your your thumb on the keys and your other fingers on the side.
- Using your nails to strike the keys will minimize finger pain and make the sound more crisp.
- Use your middle finger to cover the hole on the back to create a WAH sound.
- Train your thumb to move easily between all the keys on each side.

NOTES AND STICKERS

It will be useful if the keys of your
instrument have letter notations on
the keys.
Usually, these stickers are sold
together with the kalimba,
if not, you just need
to get and apply any
stickers with the letters.

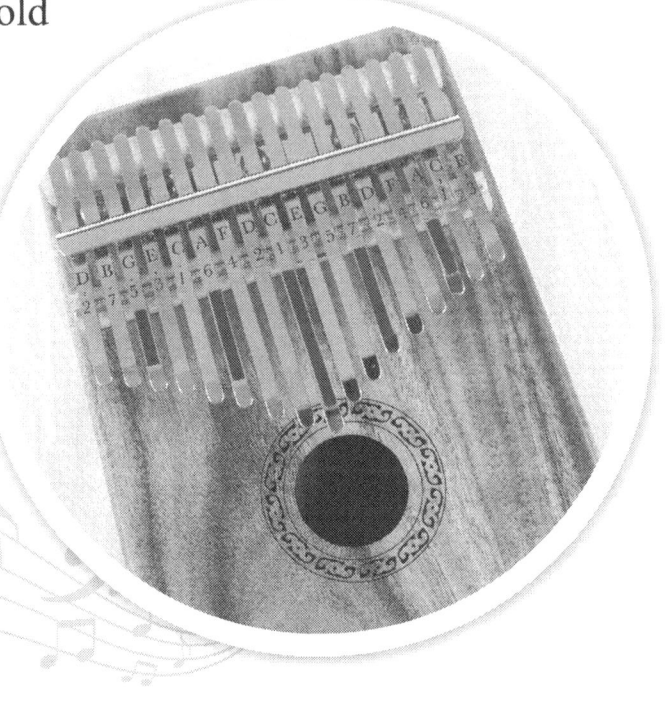

Usually, the chords for the accompaniment are written under
the notes. We write the note names, because our sheet music
is aimed at very beginners.

KtabS is a music notation system which was written especially
for the kalimba. You can find this in most places and this notation can easily be read. However, we suggest that the easiest
way to begin is to play with the letter notes in our book.

Each tab should match the number of tines on your kalimba. For example, if your kalimba has 8 tines, you need to search for "8-note kalimba tabs."

Our sheet music is not for a specific kalimba, but it is universal and suitable for 8-17 note kalimbas.

The low notes are usually in the center of a kalimba. The notes become higher as you move away from the center. The order of the notes alternate from right to left, going outward as you move up the scale. Taking "Do Re Mi Fa So La Ti Do", "Do" is on the right side, and then you will find "Re" on the left.

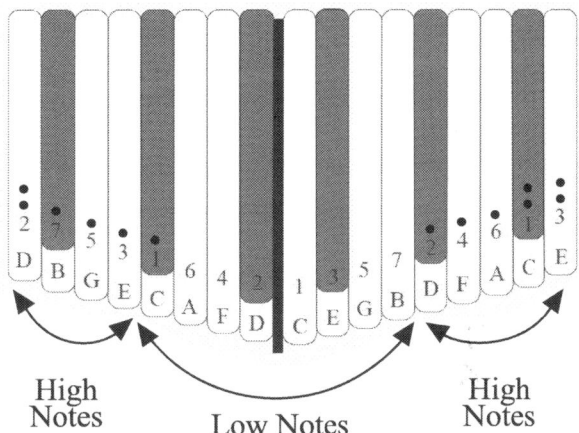

Also, the modern kalimba usually has enlarged letters representing the name of the notes. Often under the enlarged letter (or above the numbers), you can find one or two dots. These dots indicate the octave. Most kalimbas usually involve fourth, fifth and sixth octaves, and therefore can produce a high sound.

The central (the fourth normally) octave has no dots under the letters, the second (in reality fifth) is represented by one dot, and the third (sixth) has 2 dots under the letters. We also put one or two dots under the letters in the sheet music if they use an octave other than the main kalimba octave. The dots will help you to begin to play immediately.

Follow the letters… and begin to play! Usually the kalimba is considered an adult instrument, but with our visual, your kids will easily begin to play as well. Even if you or your kids don't know musical notes, you will confidently be able to play easily using the letter notation! This book might include only letters and it will be enough to begin to play, but we decided to add classic note symbols to help teach them and show musical notation.

If you are an absolute newcomer, our pictured illustration about musical notation symbols at the end of the book will help you.

Contents

Part 1

Follow the letter and music notes. Pay attention to the musical notation.

Skip, Skip, Skip to My Lou

Humpty Dumpty

My Hat

My hat it has three cor-ners, Three cor-ners has my hat, And

had it not three cor-ners, _____ it would not be my hat. _____

4

I Like to Eat
(Apples and Bananas)

Cobbler, Mend My Shoe

Lost My Gold Ring

Jamaican folk song

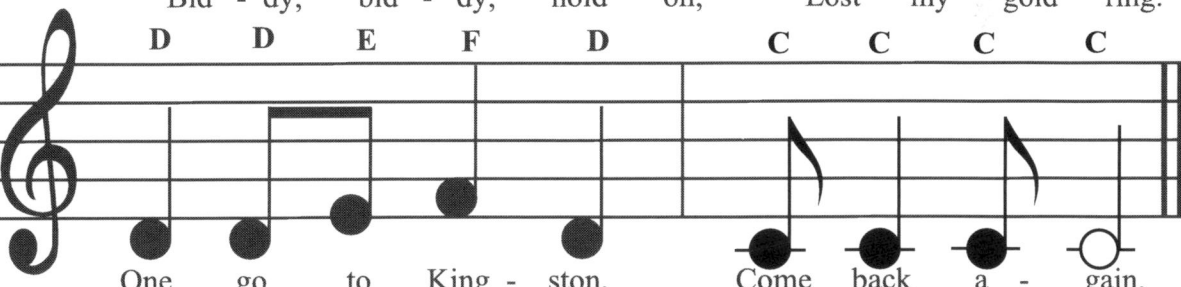

Bid - dy, bid - dy, hold on, Lost my gold ring.

One go to King - ston, Come back a - gain.

Bid - dy, bid - dy, hold on, Lost my gold ring.

One go to King - ston, Come back a - gain.

7

This Old Man

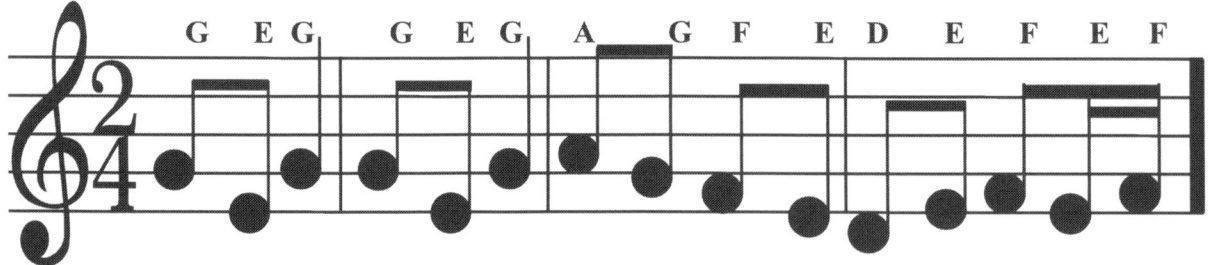

This old man, he played one, He played knick-knack on my thumb; With a

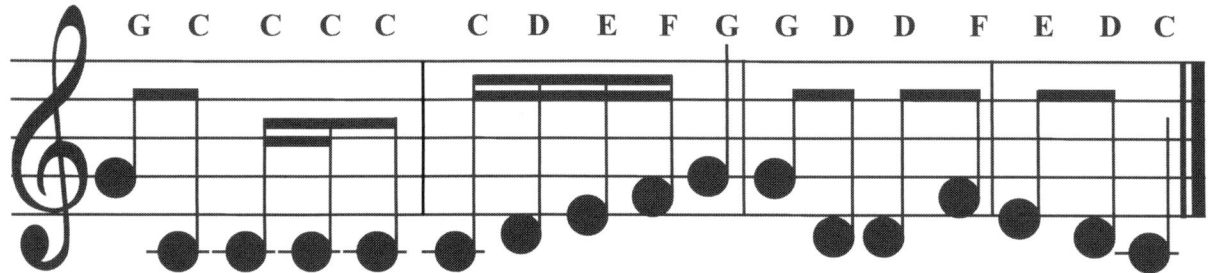

knick-knack pad- dy whack, Give the dog a bone! This old man came roll-ing home.

Baby Bumble Bee

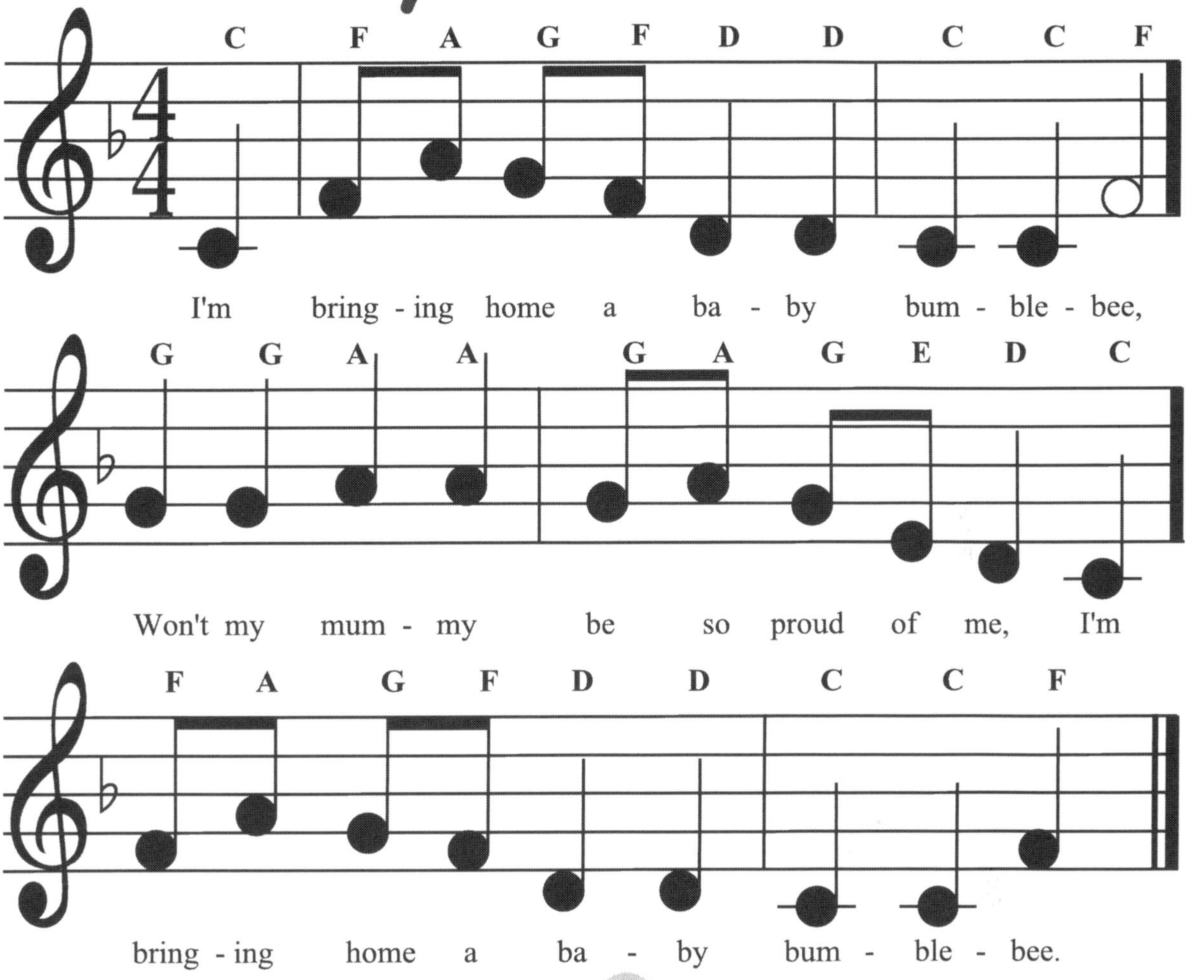

C   F   A   G   F   D   D   C   C   F

I'm   bring - ing   home   a   ba - by   bum - ble - bee,

G   G   A   A   G   A   G   E   D   C

Won't my   mum - my   be   so   proud   of   me,   I'm

F   A   G   F   D   D   C   C   F

bring - ing   home   a   ba - by   bum - ble - bee.

9

The Bear Went Over the Mountain

Cherry Blossom

Japanese folk song

*This is the most challenging song in the book.
It involves the 5th and 6th octave.*

11

Ring Around the Rosie

Rain, Rain, Go Away

A Ram Sam Sam

Little Jack Horner

It's Raining

It's rain - ing, it's pour - ing, the old man is snor - ing.

Went to bed and he bumped his head and he could -n't get up in the morn - ing.

Au Clair de la Lune

By the light of the moon, My friend Pier - rot,

Please lend me your quill pen. Just to write a word.

My candle is dead now and I have no light left.

O - pen your door for me For the love of God.

17

Debka Hora

Israeli folk song

My Bonnie

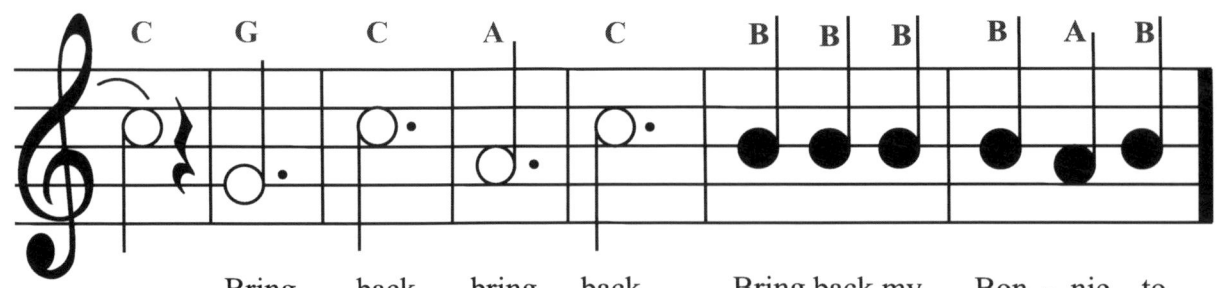

Bring back, bring back. Bring back my Bon - nie to

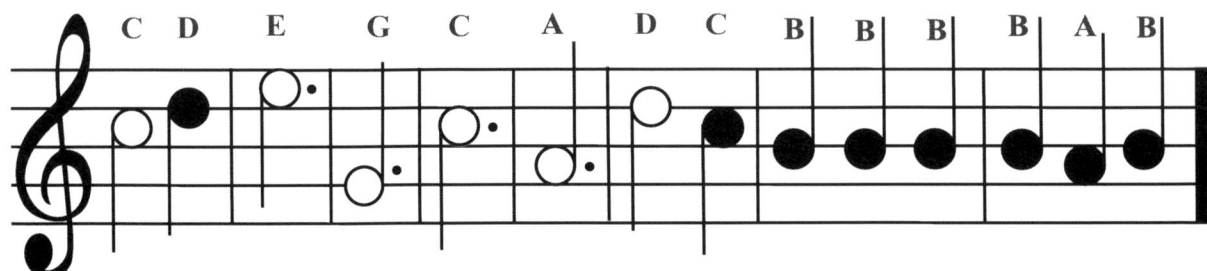

me, to me! Bring back, bring back. Oh, bring back my Bon-nie to

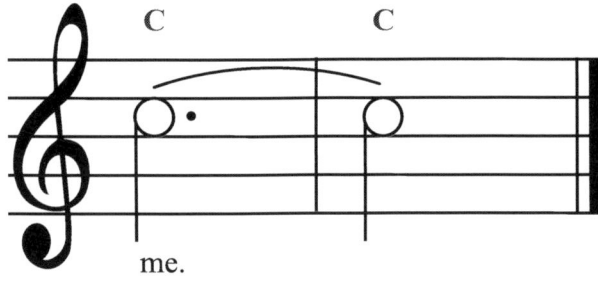

me.

My Bonnie is over the ocean
My Bonnie is over the sea
My Bonnie is over the ocean
Oh, bring back my Bonnie to me
Bring back, bring back
Oh, bring back my Bonnie to me, to me!
Bring back, bring back
Oh, bring back my Bonnie to me

20

House of the Rising Sun

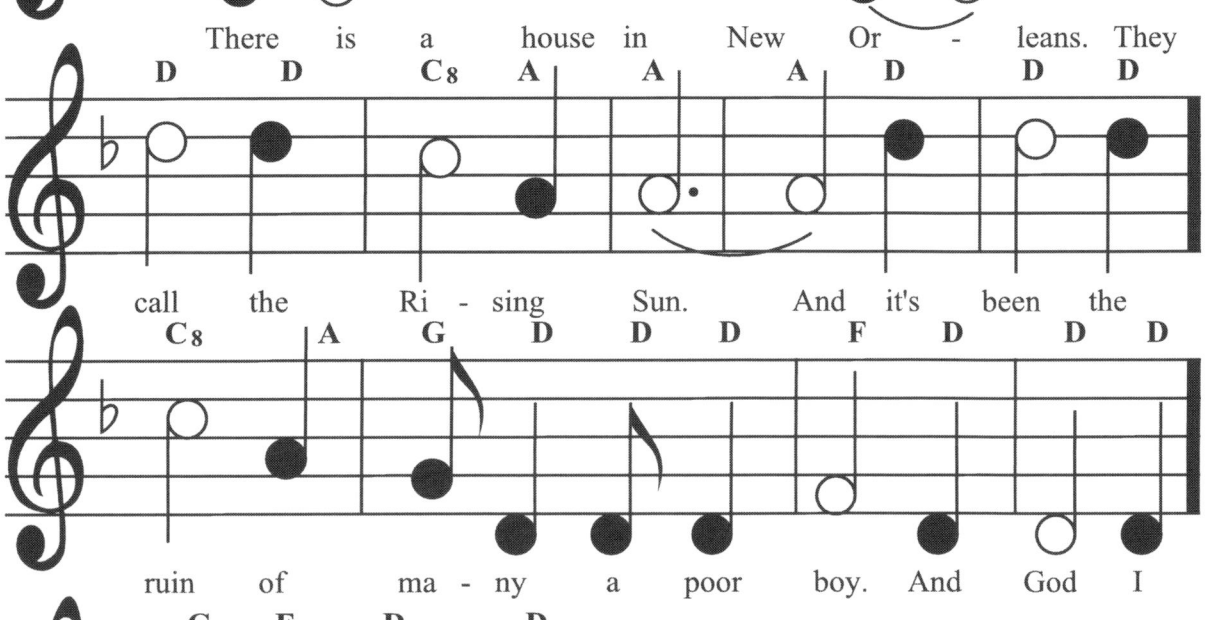

There is a house in New Orleans
They call the Rising Sun
And it's been the ruin of many a poor boy
And God I know I'm one

My mother was a tailor
She sewed my new blue jeans
My father was a gamblin' man
Down in New Orleans

Now the only thing a gambler needs
Is a suitcase and trunk
And the only time he's satisfied
Is when he's all drunk

Oh mother tell your children
Not to do what I have done
Spend your lives in sin and misery
In the House of the Rising Sun

Well, I got one foot on the platform
The other foot on the train
I'm goin' back to New Orleans
To wear that ball and chain

Well, there is a house in New Orleans
They call the Rising Sun
And it's been the ruin of many a poor boy
And God I know I'm one

21

Part 2

Here you will find 3 different songs with the same set of notes,
but with different notations.
Have you ever noticed that Twinkle Twinkle Little Star, the Alphabet Song
and Baa, Baa, Black Sheep have the same melody?
Yes, they are all based on a tune by Mozart, which is from a French tune,
"Ah, vous dirai-je, maman" ("Ah! Would I tell you, mother?").
This is good material for understanding the importance of musical notations.

Baa Baa Black Sheep

Twinkle, Twinkle, Little Star

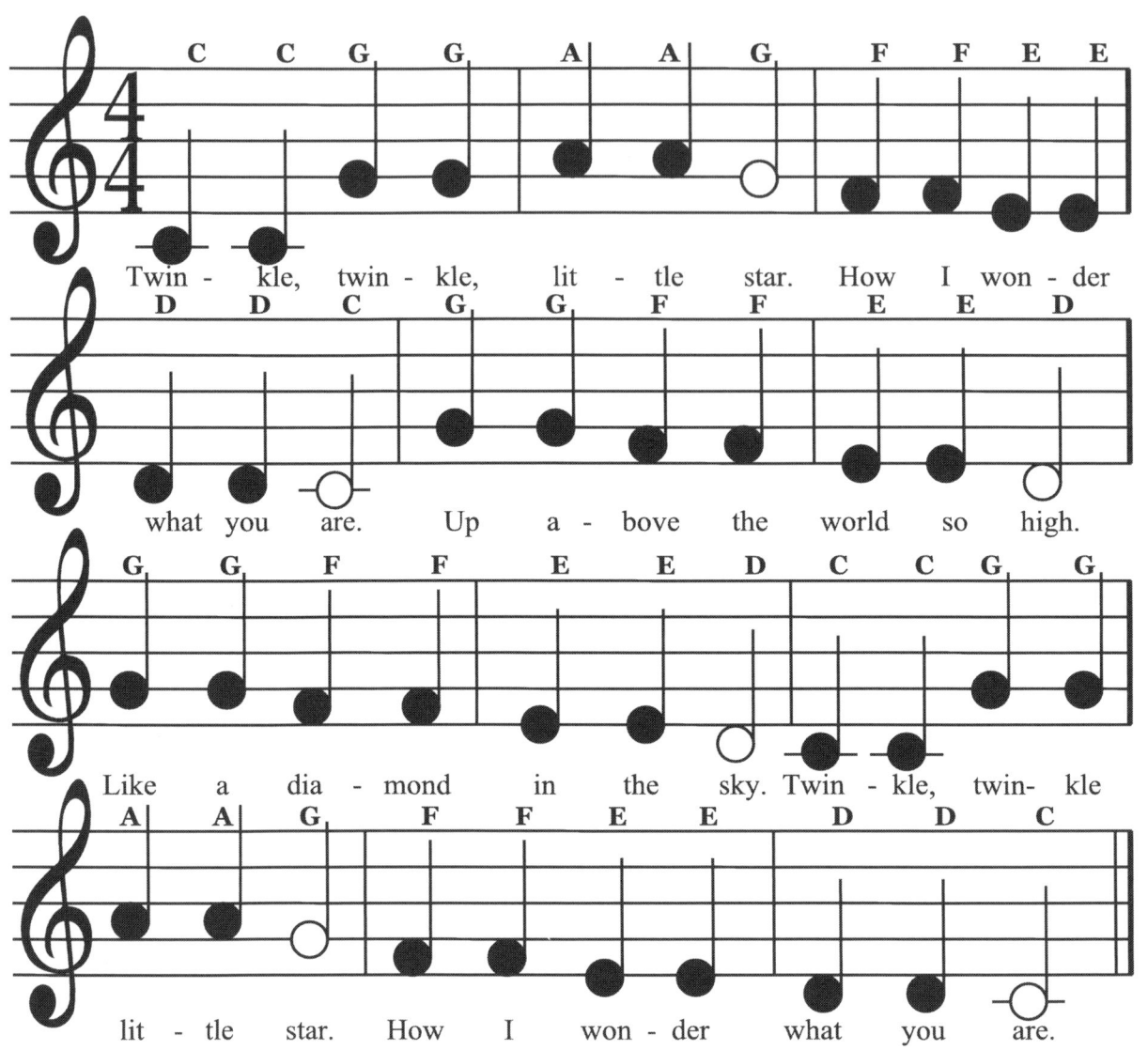

Alphabet Song

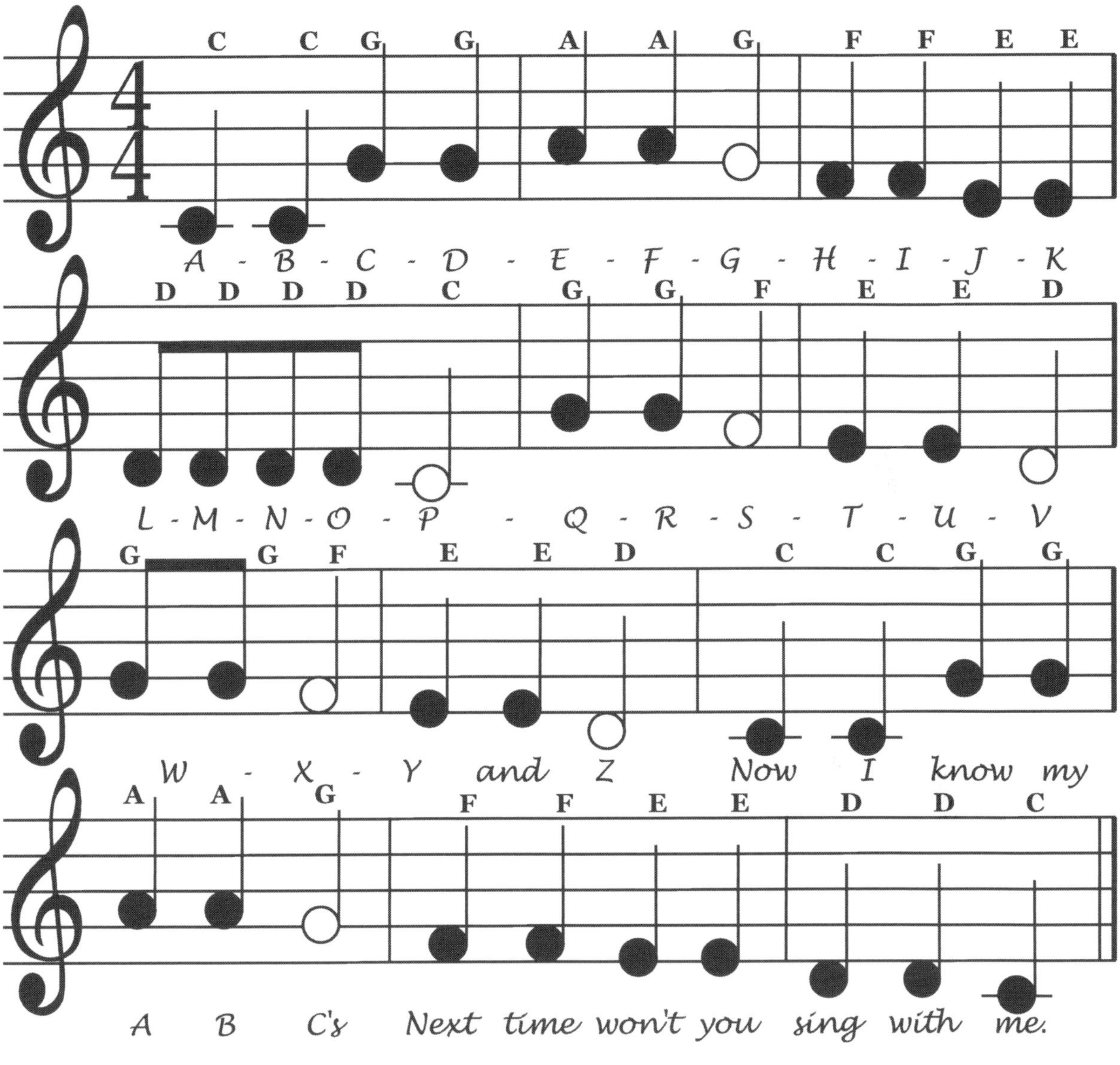

C · C · G · G · A · A · G · F · F · E · E
A - B - C - D - E - F - G - H - I - J - K

D · D · D · D · C · G · G · F · E · E · D
L - M - N - O - P - Q - R - S - T - U - V

G · G · F · E · E · D · C · C · G · G
W · A - X · G - Y · and · Z · Now · I · know · my

A · A · G · F · F · E · E · D · D · C
A · B · C's · Next time won't you sing with me.

25

Music Note Values

How to Read Music

The empty HEAD   The full HEAD

The STEM
is attached to the note head

The FLAG
must always be on the right side

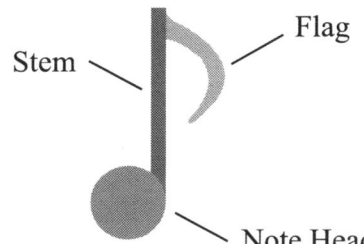

Stems may point up   **or down**

THE STAFF - The notes are named after the first seven letters of the alphabet (A to G). The name and pitch of the note is indicated by its position on five horizontal lines and spaces between.

```
——————————— 5th LINE ———————————
                                    4th SPACE
——————————— 4th LINE ———————————
                                    3rd SPACE
——————————— 3rd LINE ———————————
                                    2nd SPACE
—— 2nd LINE ——
                                    1st SPACE
—1st LINE ———————————
```

NOTES ON THE LINES   NOTES IN THE SPACES

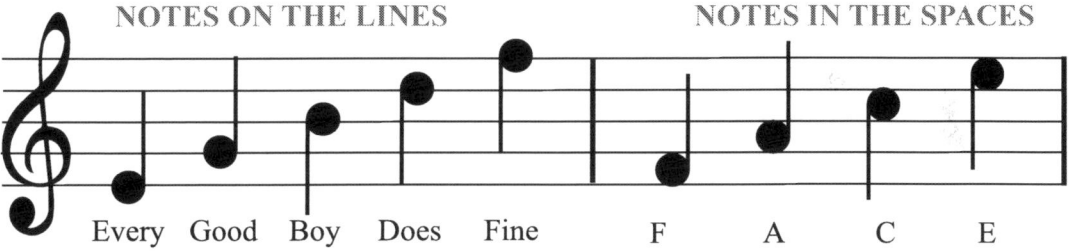

Every   Good   Boy   Does   Fine   F   A   C   E

TREBLE CLEF

The treble clef, also called the G clef, shows that the second line is the note G.

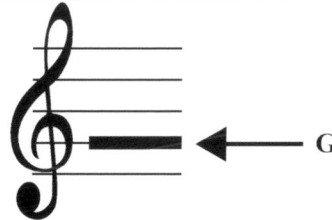

DOTTED NOTE

A dot indicates that the note should be held for an additional half of the note's beat.

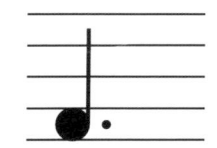

TIE

A pair of tied notes indicates that the two beats are played as one extended note.

Bar

Bar (or measure)
A bar contains a specific number of beats within bar lines.

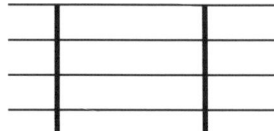

Double Bar
A double bar line shows the end of a piece of music.

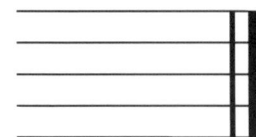

REPEAT SIGNS

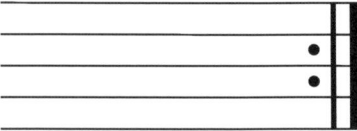

Go back to the beginning of the song and play again.

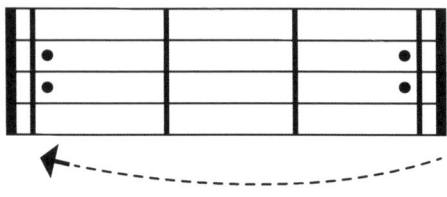

Go back to the "begin repeat" sign and play again.

Time Signature

Time signatures are used to specify how many beats are contained in each measure of music, and which note value is equivalent to one beat.

Number of beats per measure.

What type of note gets one beat.

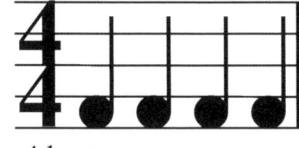

4 = 4 beats per measure
4 = quarter note gets 1 beat

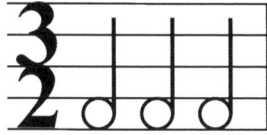

3 = 3 beats per measure
2 = half note gets 1 beat

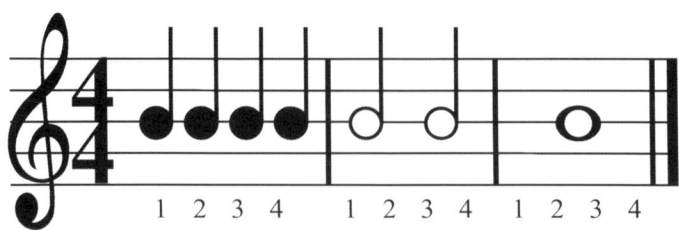

1 2 3 4   1 2 3 4   1 2 3 4

Made in the USA
Monee, IL
18 November 2021

82486800R00022